D1162897

STARS OF SPORTS

KAWHI LEONARD

PRO BASKETBALL CHAMPION

by Shane Frederick

CAPSTONE PRESS
a capstone imprint

Stars of Sports is published by Capstone Press, an imprint of Capstone.
1710 Roe Crest Drive, North Mankato, Minnesota 56003
www.capstonepub.com

Copyright © 2020 by Capstone Press, an imprint of Capstone. All rights reserved.
No part of this publication may be reproduced in whole or in part, or stored in a
retrieval system, or transmitted in any form or by any means, electronic, mechanical,
photocopying, recording, or otherwise, without written permission of the publisher.

**Library of Congress Cataloging-in-Publication Data is available on the Library
of Congress website.**
ISBN: 978-1-4966-8379-3 (hardcover)
ISBN: 978-1-4966-8430-1 (eBook PDF)

Summary: Kawhi "the Klaw" Leonard is a well-known name in basketball. At a
towering height of 6 feet, 7 inches, Leonard is one of the most dominant defenders
in the NBA. Leonard was just 20 years old when he was first drafted into the NBA.
Since then he has had many triumphs and has helped lead his teams to greatness.
Discover more about Leonard's career highlights in this exciting biography in the
Stars of Sports series.

Editorial Credits
Editor: Anna Butzer; Designer: Sarah Bennett; Media Researcher: Eric Gohl;
Production Specialist: Laura Manthe

Image Credits
Newscom: Cal Sport Media/Louis Lopez, 8, 9, Icon SMI/Derrick Tuskan, 10, 11, 13,
Icon Sportswire/Brian Rothmuller, cover, 27, 28, KRT/Ron Cortes, 7, Reuters/Mike
Stone, 15, USA Today Sports, 24, USA Today Sports/Bob Donnan, 17, USA Today
Sports/Jaime Valdez, 21, USA Today Sports/John E. Sokolowski, 22, USA Today
Sports/Soobum Im, 18, 19, ZUMA Press/Edward A. Ornelas, 16, ZUMA Press/Pi/
Javier Rojas, 5; Shutterstock: Oleksii Sidorov, 1

All internet sites appearing in back matter were available and accurate when this
book was sent to press.

Direct Quotations

Page 9, "Basketball is my life . . ." Nick Jungfer, "How a Gutting Family Tragedy
Made Kawhi Leonard Who He is," June 12, 2019, https://basketballforever.
com/2019/06/12/how-a-gutting-family-tragedy-made-kawhi-leonard-who-he-is.
Accessed on November 11, 2019.
Page 10, "We've never had a guy . . ." Ben Bolch, "Spurs' Kawhi Leonard Has
Prevailed in Tough Times," June 11, 2014, https://www.latimes.com/sports/la-sp-
heat-spurs-nba-finals-20140612-story.html.
Accessed on November 11, 2019.

Printed in the United States of America.
PA117

TABLE OF CONTENTS

Glossary terms are **BOLD** on first use.

WINNER-WINNER

In 2019, the Toronto Raptors made it to the National Basketball Association (NBA) Finals. They had never made it this far. But they had never had a superstar like Kawhi Leonard before, either.

The Raptors faced the mighty Golden State Warriors. The Warriors had won three of the previous four NBA championships. They were hungry to win another title.

Although the experience was new to the Raptors, it wasn't new to Leonard. In 2014, he had led the San Antonio Spurs to an NBA championship.

With Leonard leading the way, the Raptors shocked the basketball world. They knocked off the Warriors four games to two. When it was over, Leonard was named Most Valuable Player (MVP) of the NBA Finals for the second time in his career!

<<< Kawhi Leonard (2) puts up a shot over his opponent from the Golden State Warriors.

Kawhi Leonard was born on June 29, 1991, in Los Angeles, California. He was the youngest of five children. He and his four older sisters grew up in the city of Moreno Valley.

There are two NBA teams in Los Angeles, the Lakers and the Clippers. Leonard wasn't a fan of either team, though. Instead, he liked the Philadelphia 76ers and their star player, Allen Iverson.

Iverson was a 6-foot (183-centimeter) point guard. Leonard, a small forward, grew up to be 6 feet, 7 inches (201 cm) tall. He became a much different kind of player from his idol.

Leonard went to Canyon Springs High School. As a freshman, he did not play for the basketball team. It wasn't because he wasn't good enough. His mom wasn't able to give her son a ride to the gym for tryouts. The coach was strict about tryouts. He kept Leonard off the team.

‹‹‹ Allen Iverson
played in the NBA
for 14 years.

Leonard finally made the basketball team as a sophomore. After one year there, he moved to Martin Luther King High School in Riverside, California. He played his final two years of high school basketball there. He worked hard to improve his game. In 2009, he was so good, he was named California's Mr. Basketball.

Leonard made great strides during his two years playing for Martin Luther King High School.

Missing Support

Leonard's father, Mark Leonard, died suddenly in 2008. Heartbroken, Kawhi still played in a game the next day. He scored 17 points. Afterward, he cried in the arms of his mother, Kim. "Basketball is my life," he said, "and I wanted to go out there and take my mind off it. It was real sad. My father was supposed to be at the game."

During high school, Leonard wasn't **recruited** by many big-time college programs. San Diego State University liked him, though. In 2009, the school offered him a scholarship to play as an Aztec.

At San Diego State, Kawhi continued to work on his skills. Oftentimes he would go to the gym early in the morning by himself. "We've never had a guy that's put more gym time in when nobody's watching, when it's not required," Aztecs coach Steve Fisher said. "Nobody."

>>> Leonard (right) playing for the Aztecs in February 2010.

The hard work paid off. During his two seasons with the Aztecs, Leonard had 40 **double-doubles**. He **averaged** 14.1 points and 10.2 rebounds per game. San Diego State won two Mountain West **Conference** tournament championships while Leonard was there.

During his second season, Leonard led the Aztecs to a school-record 34 wins. San Diego State earned a spot in the NCAA tournament. The Aztecs won two games in the tournament to advance to the regional semifinals. They were one of 16 remaining teams. In the Sweet 16, the Aztecs lost to the University of Connecticut. Connecticut went on to win the national title. But Leonard had made his mark.

FACT

Leonard was called "the Claw" or "the Klaw" in high school because of his massive hands. They measure 11.25 inches (28.5 cm) from pinky to thumb and are 9.75 inches (24.7 cm) long. His big hands help him steal the ball. They also help grab rebounds at both ends of the court.

After his second season, Leonard decided that he was ready for the NBA. He announced that he was going to skip his final two years of college basketball and enter the 2011 NBA **draft**. The Indiana Pacers drafted Leonard with the 15th overall pick. But the Pacers traded him to the San Antonio Spurs later that same night.

Leonard joined a very good Spurs team. San Antonio had become an NBA powerhouse with coach Gregg Popovich. The team also had superstar center Tim Duncan leading the way. The Spurs had already won championships in 1999, 2003, 2005, and 2007. Two more stars, Tony Parker and Manu Ginobili, were on the last three of those title teams. Leonard hoped to help them win again.

During his **rookie** season, Leonard started a little more than half of the Spurs' games. He averaged just 7.9 points and 5.1 rebounds per game. But he still made the NBA's 2011–2012 All-Rookie Team. He continued to put in extra time in the gym. He stayed late after practice to work on his footwork, ball-handling, and three-point shot.

⟩⟩⟩ Leonard (2) dunks the ball during a game against the Utah Jazz in 2012.

Leonard's hard work paid off. He became a starter in his second season as a Spur. By the end of that season, he helped the Spurs make it to the NBA Finals. They battled LeBron James and the Miami Heat in a series that went all seven games. The Spurs ended up losing four games to three. But Leonard was determined to win.

In the 2013–2014 season, the Spurs once again made it to the Finals. They faced LeBron and the Miami Heat again. Miami was going for a third straight championship. The Spurs team wasn't much different from the one that had lost to the Heat a year earlier. But there was one big difference—Kawhi Leonard was starting to take over.

〉〉〉 Leonard (right) moves around the Miami Heat's LeBron James during Game 3 of the NBA Finals in 2014.

FACT

At 22 years old, Leonard was the third-youngest NBA Finals MVP. He was the youngest since the Lakers' Magic Johnson. Johnson had won it in 1980, when he was 20 years old.

Leonard averaged 17.8 points and 6.4 rebounds per game in the Finals. More importantly, he was a force on defense. There his job was to shut down LeBron James. The Spurs stunned the Heat. They won four games to one. Leonard was named Finals MVP!

Leonard continued to get better for the Spurs over his next four seasons. He had become one of the Spurs' best players. But he had also gained a spot as one of the NBA's best players. He was named First Team All-NBA in 2016 and 2017. During those two seasons, he averaged about 23 points per game. He was also named the Defensive Player of the Year in 2015 and 2016.

>>> Leonard (2) dunks the ball over his opponents during a game in May 2017.

Leonard couldn't get the Spurs back to the NBA Finals, however. The Golden State Warriors were one big reason for that. Another was an injury. During Game 1 of the 2017 Western Conference Finals against the Warriors, Kawhi hurt his ankle. He had to sit out the rest of the series. Golden State ended up sweeping the Spurs in four games.

Leonard's injury lingered during the next season. He played just nine games. He was also becoming unhappy in San Antonio. He wanted to play for a new team.

After the 2018 season, Leonard asked the Spurs to trade him. He wanted to be traded to a team in his hometown of Los Angeles, so either the Lakers or the Clippers. The Spurs agreed to trade him, but they didn't want to compete with him in the Western Conference. They opted to send him east instead, to the Toronto Raptors.

The Raptors were one of the best teams in the Eastern Conference. They had star players including DeMar DeRozan and Kyle Lowry. However, they couldn't get past the Cleveland Cavaliers, who now had star player LeBron James. The Cavs had knocked the Raptors out of the playoffs for three years in a row. But Leonard would soon change their luck.

‹‹‹ Though Kawhi Leonard switched from the Spurs to the Raptors, he was able to keep his jersey number the same.

>>> Leonard's teammates watch as he launches his buzzer-beating shot.

THE RAPTORS RALLY

Leonard helped Toronto to a great season in 2018–2019. The Raptors went 58–24. Leonard averaged 26.6 points, 7.3 rebounds, and 3.3 assists per game along the way.

The Raptors finished second in the tough Eastern Conference. They hoped they could finally make it to the NBA Finals.

The Raptors breezed through the first round of playoffs, defeating the Orlando Magic four games to one. The second round against the 76ers was tougher. But Leonard got them through, making an all-time great shot to win Game 7.

He made a **buzzer-beater** from the right corner to win the game. The ball bounced on the rim four times before finally going through the hoop! This shot sent the Raptors on to the conference finals.

In the conference finals, the Raptors faced the Bucks. The Bucks had their own superstar player, Giannis Antetokounmpo. The Bucks were heavily favored. They won the first two games of the series. It looked like they would be moving on to the NBA Finals. But Leonard was not about to go away quietly.

Over the next four games, Leonard averaged nearly 30 points per game. The Raptors won each of those games and rocketed past the Bucks to the NBA Finals.

>>> Leonard dribbles the ball past Milwaukee Bucks' superstar player Giannis Antetokounmpo.

FACT

Kawhi Leonard is one of three players to be named NBA Finals MVP for two different teams (Spurs and Raptors). The others were LeBron James (Heat, Cavaliers) and Kareem Abdul-Jabbar (Bucks, Lakers).

The 2019 NBA Finals were set. It would be the Raptors versus Warriors. The Warriors had a star-studded lineup that included Stephen Curry, Kevin Durant, Draymond Green, and Klay Thompson. As good as those players were, Leonard was about to prove he was even better.

Over the next six games, he averaged 28.5 points. He also averaged 9.8 rebounds, 4.2 assists, 2.0 steals, and 1.2 blocks. The Raptors celebrated a 114–110 victory in Game 6. They had earned their first NBA championship!

After the 2019 Finals, Leonard's contract with the Raptors had expired. He was a **free agent**. He was able to sign with any team in the NBA.

The Raptors wanted him back, in hopes of winning another championship. Their fans begged him to return. They made crazy offers to try to convince him to stay. Toronto restaurants said he could eat for free for the rest of his life. He was even offered a luxurious condo to live in.

But Leonard decided he wanted to go home to Southern California. He signed a three-year contract with the Los Angeles Clippers. There would be just one magical season with the Raptors.

Giving Back

Before playing his first game with the Clippers, Leonard did something big for the people of Southern California. He went to his elementary school in his hometown of Moreno Valley. There he announced he was donating 1 million backpacks to students.

SEEKING ANOTHER TITLE

The Clippers have always been in the shadow of Los Angeles' other team, the Lakers. The Lakers have won 16 championships. They have also had superstars such as Magic Johnson, Kareem Abdul-Jabbar, Kobe Bryant, and Shaquille O'Neal. In 2018, they signed LeBron James.

Meanwhile, the Clippers have never won a championship. In fact, they have never advanced past the second round of the playoffs.

But the Raptors had never won a title before Kawhi Leonard arrived, either. Perhaps it will be "the Klaw" who leads the Clippers to their first NBA title.

TIMELINE

1991   Kawhi Leonard is born in Los Angeles, California

2009   Leonard is named California's Mr. Basketball; begins playing at San Diego State University

2011   Leads Aztecs to NCAA Sweet 16; enters NBA Draft, is picked by Indiana and traded to San Antonio

2012   Makes NBA All-Rookie Team

2014   Named NBA Finals MVP as Spurs win championship

2015   Wins the first of two NBA Defensive Player of the Year awards

2018   Traded to Toronto

2019   Named Finals MVP again as Raptors win championship; signs with L.A. Clippers

GLOSSARY

AVERAGE (AV-uh-rij)—taking a player's total stats in a season and dividing them by the number of games

BUZZER-BEATER (buzz-uhr-BEET-uhr)—a score that takes place just as time runs out

CONFERENCE (KAHN-fuhr-uhns)—a group of sports teams that play against each other

DOUBLE-DOUBLE (DUH-buhl-DUH-buhl)—having more than 10 in two statistical categories, such as points and rebounds

DRAFT (DRAFT)—an event in which professional teams select new players

FREE AGENT (FREE AY-juhnt)—a player who is free to sign with any team

RECRUITED (ri-KROO-ted)—having found players to join a college team

ROOKIE (RUK-ee)—a player in his or her first year

READ MORE

Bryant, Howard. *Legends: The Best Players, Games, and Teams in Basketball.* New York: Philomel Books, 2017.

Peterson, Megan Cooley. *Basketball's Great Players.* North Mankato, MN: Black Rabbit Books, 2017.

Williams, Heather. *Basketball: A Guide for Players and Fans.* North Mankato, MN: Capstone Press, 2020.

INTERNET SITES

Basketball Hall of Fame
www.hoophall.com

Basketball Reference
www.basketball-reference.com

National Basketball Association
www.nba.com

INDEX